The Cybernetic Possum

Published in the United States of America
By Spinoza Publishing
5310 Healy Lane
Monona, WI 53716

www.spinozapublishing.com

ISBN: 978-0-9789-093-1-4

First Edition

Cover design by Danny Torres
Drawings by Richard Chamberlin

The Cybernetic Possum

A Collection of Short Stories and Poems
With a tribute to Greg Knutson

By

Richard Chamberlin

SPINOZA PUBLISHING
Monona, Wisconsin

Acknowledgements

I want to thank my wife Judi Torres for helping typeset this book and Aaron Shepard, the author of *Perfect Pages* for teaching us how to use Microsoft Word to do it. Thanks also to my sisters, Sandra Chamberlin Michaels and Bette Chamberlin, for encouraging me to publish my short works. I also want to thank my stepson Danny Torres for helping design the cover. His computer wizardry was invaluable. Special thanks go to Richard Knutson for coming through at the last minute with a picture of his brother Greg.

Other books by Richard Chamberlin

Contents

Introduction

Over the years I've accumulated many writings and poems that were birthed into existence for one reason or another, read to a few friends then placed into the collected unconsciousness of boxes and files.

This collection contains five short stories and 24 poems from those boxes and files. Many of the poems were written during a six-month period in 1992 when I tasked myself with writing a poem a day. Of those, these are the ones I liked best. Other poems were written over the years anytime the spirit grabbed me.

I wrote the poem *Hey Baby!* as part of a project by the Wisconsin Humanities Council. Poets were asked to write about exhibits at the Elvehjem (now the Chazen) Art Museum in Madison, Wisconsin. As soon as I entered the gallery my eye was drawn to the sculpture of a realistic looking naked woman sitting on the floor. The depth of detail was amazing. I was going through a lonely period in my life and wished the statue would suddenly come to life. I scribbled down a few lines of my initial impressions at the museum then fleshed the rest out at home. Later all the poems were read in front of each work of art by a museum docent as part of a special tour in which the public was invited.

The Cybernetic Possum was written in 1973 while I was a newspaper reporter on a small newspaper in Northern Indiana. It has been published in *The State* newspaper in Columbia, South Carolina and also in Madison's *Isthmus.* About a year ago I found an injured baby possum on the east side bicycle path while riding to work. I put it into my backpack and took it to a wild animal hospital but unfortunately it didn't survive.

The Cybernetic Possum

Several stories and poems (*Ralph Nader Comes to Madison*, *Bucks Tavern*, *An Inside Job*, *Wars Never End*, and *Hacking It*) are about my experiences driving for Union Cab in Madison since 1982. A number of people have made a lasting impression on me and I always enjoy sharing their stories with others.

The Honest Thief was written in 1975 after I returned from a hitchhiking trip to California. The prose version of that experience appears in Chapter 28 of my memoir, *Hitchhiking from Vietnam: Seeking the Ox* published in 2007 by Spinoza Publishing. The short story *Rocky Mountain High* was deleted from the same memoir which already had two LSD trips in it. Here is the third.

I entered the story *The Purple Lion* in *The Plot Quickens,* a 24-hour writing contest in 2003 that was sponsored by the *Capital Times* and the Wisconsin Book Festival. The assignment was: "Something's happening here. What is it? What comes next? Or what came before it?" The contest used photographer William Gedney's *Girl Lost in Thought at Fast Food Counter* for inspiration. I didn't win the contest but was pleased with myself for completing the story in only 24-hours.

Finally, I've included six poems by Greg Knutson who used to drive and dispatch for Union Cab Cooperative of Madison. Greg was a gentle spirit, a kind of Renaissance man who was a guitarist, poet and National Chess Master who was working on his PhD in Mathematics at The University of Wisconsin. He died in 1996 at the age of 37 after being struck by a car on the interstate highway north of Madison.

Short Stories

Ralph Nader Visits Madison

One of the perks of driving cab is every now and then giving a ride to someone famous. That happened on November 1, 2000 when Ralph Nader was making his last campaign swing through Wisconsin before the presidential election. I was selected to be one of two Union Cab drivers to shuttle him around Madison for a noon rally at the Capitol followed by an appearance at the Orpheum Theater. From there we would take him to Milwaukee.

I admired Nader for having the guts to challenge the two-party system and voted for him in 1996. To me, he represented the best hope of the people to rescue their government from corporate control. He was one of my heroes.

The night before he was to arrive I had trouble falling asleep anticipating what would happen. Would he even be riding with me? If he did there were any number of things we could talk about-his life, my life, the environment, corporate control of the government-the list was endless. What a great discussion we could have.

I wasn't familiar with the streets in Milwaukee but got some cursory directions from the dispatcher. When we pulled our yellow mini-vans into Madison's airport late that morning my green *Nader/La Duke* button was pinned to my yellow Union Cab T-shirt. Shortly before noon, two very large men in suits and sunglasses emerged from the terminal and walked over to my van. One opened the front passenger door then both men posted themselves near the van, in the wide stanched military "parade rest" position.

"Are you with the Nader group?" I asked.

"Stay inside," ordered the large black man standing next to the front door. Just then several people exited the terminal and began walking toward my van. One of them was Ralph Nader dressed in a dark suit. He was talking and holding a stack of papers in one hand and a bottle of spring water in the other.

He climbed in next to me without even saying hello. He was holding a press release about the Crandon Mine which was being proposed in northern Wisconsin and began cross-examining his aids. "Is this verified?" he asked pointedly. "We've got to get this verified."

When I had seen him on TV he looked haggard with slumped shoulders but now he looked tanned and younger than I had expected. Since he had not even acknowledged my presence I decided to try and make contact. Something simple, I thought. I didn't want to monopolize his time.

Everyone was calling him Ralph but it didn't seem appropriate to get that informal, at least not until we'd had time to talk.

He pulled the door shut and turned slightly toward me. "Welcome to Madison, Mr. Nader," I said.

He glanced over, gave me a half smile and said, "Thanks."

We left the airport and drove toward the Capitol. I had been in Crandon, Wisconsin for the demonstration against Exxon's proposed mine few years earlier. I had watched as Nader's Wisconsin campaign manager, Ben Manski, got slammed to the hood of a police car, handcuffed, and hauled off to jail. I thought that maybe I could make the issue come alive for Nader by relating my personal experience.

"I was up in Crandon protesting that mine a couple years ago," I began. "A lot of people got arrested."

"Is the site on public land or is it private?" asked Nader.

"Exxon used to own it then they sold it to Rio Tinto Zinc, now I'm not sure who owns it…" I said trying to remember the tangled mess of ownerships. Suddenly his aid handed Nader the cell phone. To my disappointment he was talking on it all the way downtown.

When we arrived at the domed Capitol building police waved us into two narrow parking spaces on the East Washington Avenue entrance. Nader, the body guards and his aids got out of my van and the reporters got out of the other.

One of the bodyguards, who had the physique of an ex-football lineman, ordered us to turn our vans around facing the street and to stay with them. I resented being told I had to stay with my van. I had been planning to attend the rally for a week and thought this would be the perfect opportunity to get paid while doing it. I snuck a peek of the rally anyway.

At about 1:30 pm Nader returned.

"CNN screwed us," he said to someone in the back. "They said we had only 500 people there. How many people would you say?"

"I'd say about two thousand," said the bodyguard.

"Yeah, about two thousand," I said but no one paid any attention to me.

We drove a couple blocks to the back of the Orpheum Theater where Nader was taping the interview with Chris Matthews of MSNBC in front of a live audience of rabid supporters.

"Turn the vans around facing out," commanded the bodyguard. Nader and most everyone else went in through the stage door. A black bodyguard stayed behind. He walked a few steps away from the van, lit a cigarette and began scanning the parking ramp. I decided to try and make friends.

I walked over to him. "What's your name?"

"Leonard," he said.

"Hi, I'm Richard." We shook hands.

"So where are you from," I asked.

"Arizona."

"Been with Nader a long time?"

"No, just a few days," he said as he continued scanning the ramp.

"Are you with the Secret Service?"

"No, we're private."

"So have there been any threats to Nader ?"

"No," replied Leonard. He took a drag on his cigarette, glanced at me out of the corner of his eyes and backed away.

I returned to the van and waited as Adam Chern, the other driver, ran down State Street to buy a couple books for Nader to sign. He returned with two copies of *The Ralph Nader Reader*.

At 3:30 pm Nader's road manager, a lean young man with wiry hair, stopped by and said Nader had to be in Milwaukee by 5:20 pm for a press conference. I told him we probably wouldn't make it.

"What do you mean?" he asked. "I just drove it the other day."

"Yeah, well, was it at rush hour?" I asked.

He stalked off. After Nader finished his appearance at the Orpheum he and his entourage packed into the vans and we headed out of town. Nader rode shotgun again and was on the cell phone. I was looking for the right time to ask him to autograph the books. When he got off the phone he started picking through a large sack of sandwiches in plastic containers.

"Are there any sandwiches here without meat?" he asked. "I don't eat meat."

"Here, I don't think this one has any meat," said a female aid handing him a sandwich.

There was a moment of quiet as we hit the interstate so I asked him if he could sign the books.

"Sure," he said.

The beefy bodyguard, who was seated behind me, leaned forward. In a loud, angry whisper he commanded, "Don't talk to Mr. Nader. Just keep your eyes on the road."

I thought, who does this guy think he is? He can't tell me who I can and can't talk to. It's still a free country isn't it? Besides, he was working for Ralph Nader, champion of the people.

I handed Nader the books and said, "Write one to Richard and the other to Adam."

"I told you not to talk to Mr. Nader," said the bodyguard, straining through clenched teeth.

What is he going to do? Make me pull over and slap me around? I decided to take our dispute to a higher authority.

"Mr. Nader?" I asked. "Do you mind if I talk to you? Your bodyguard seems to have a problem with that. I'm a cab driver. I talk with people all the time when I am driving."

"No I don't have any problem with that," Nader said nonchalantly before taking a bite of his sandwich. "I just can't answer because I'm eating."

"I just wanted to tell you about Union Cab," I said. It had occurred to me that Nader was completely unaware that we were a progressive company that practiced workplace democracy and stood for many of the ideals he talked about. I wanted to shake him out of this bubble of campaigning and media interviews and give him a sense of where he was. I began telling him about how we are a worker owned and operated co-op which was started after we struck Checker Cab out of business in 1978. I told him about how we were all stockholders in the co-op and elected a board of directors that could hire and fire management.

"That's great," he said. "Do you make a profit?"

I told him most of the profit is plowed back into the co-op. He nodded and seemed satisfied asking me to send him some more information.

"Excuse me Ralph," came a voice from the rear. "When you finish talking could you take a look at this press release?"

Finally some respect. I was finished.

An aide handed Nader a cell phone and soon he was giving an interview to someone in Boston. Traffic was heavy as we came into Milwaukee. I had to stop quickly a couple times for slowdowns and people cutting in front of me. Nader's campaign manager leaned forward from the bench seat behind me and said, "Drive faster. We're going to be late." I wanted to punch him. A car stopped in front of me and I slammed on the brakes.

"Don't tailgate," said Nader.

"I'm trying not to," I said.

After we began moving again I saw a sign which read, "1½ Miles To I-43." I reviewed the directions I'd been given before we left Madison- "Exit left at I-43 then make a quick right onto Kilbourne." I didn't want to miss this turn because I wasn't familiar with Milwaukee streets. I had a map somewhere in my bag but it was too late to look at it. I got into my left lane and exited onto I-43 then looked to my right and, to my horror, saw only solid traffic. I couldn't make the turn. Don't panic, I thought. *Just take the next exit.* Adam was still behind me. Nader was on the phone and no one knew I'd blown the exit. I broke into a cold sweat.

I got off at the next exit and tried to drive back toward Kilbourne but soon became lost. Luckily Adam knew where we were going and pulled in front of me. I followed him until we arrived at the Milwaukee Auditorium at about 5:45 p.m.

Nader got out and handed me his card. "Send me some information," he said and then he was gone.

The reporters, bodyguards and staff piled out of the vans leaving behind bags of uneaten gourmet sandwiches and cans of pop. Aside from the leftover food and $5 we got from the ABC news reporter, the Nader party stiffed us. We sorted through the sandwiches and had a snack before driving back to Madison.

The experience left me disillusioned with Nader so I decided to cast my vote for Vice President Gore. Later I wished that enough Florida voters had done the same.

"Girl lost in Thought at Fast Food Counter" by William Gedney ©William Gedney Collection, Duke University Rare Book Manuscript and Special Collections Library. Neg. 10267 DB NY0009.

The Purple Lion

Billy Washington was getting impatient as he sat in front of the Queens brownstone in his limo. He checked his watch. The time was 2:30 pm. There was still just enough time to drop Mrs. Palmer at her daughter's and make it to Coney Island for the five o'clock appointment with Mr. Kazantakis.

"Loosen up," Billy told himself. He closed his eyes, took a deep breath and exhaled slowly rolling his head from side to side just like his counselor had told him to do.

Suddenly he heard a loud tapping on the window.

"Wake up, wake up," shouted a heavily made up older black woman with silver hair wearing a brown fur coat.

"Sorry Mrs. Palmer," said Billy as he got out of the car to open the door for her.

"If you want to sleep do it on your own time."

Mrs. Palmer settled into the rear seat as Billy got back in. He adjusted the brim of his cap, pulled the black Cadillac limo into traffic and headed toward the Long Island Expressway. He was proud of himself for not loosing his cool with Mrs. Palmer and thought he might actually keep a job this time. It wasn't easy for a black Vietnam veteran with a drug record to get a driving job these days, but he'd been clean for two years. The Vietnam veterans' rap sessions helped and he'd begun communicating with his wife again. Now, Monique was pregnant with their first child and he wanted to be a good father. They had married after he got back from Vietnam in 1972 shortly before the flashbacks began. First came the uncontrollable shaking and then the hot flashes, followed by feelings of helplessness. The face of a young Vietnamese girl would flash before him. He was back in Dong Ha.

Members of his platoon were raping her. He shouted at the soldiers to stop. "What are you doing?" he said.

"What does it look like?" said one of the soldiers. He had his pants down and was about to rape the girl. "If you want a piece of this you've got to wait your turn." Two other soldiers held the girl's wrists. She couldn't have been more than 15 years-old.

Billie stepped forward. "It's not right," he said. A soldier pointed his M-16 at him. "Get back nigger or I'll blow your head off."

In his flashbacks he tried to help her but it was like trying to move through molasses. Sometimes the flashbacks came in the form of disembodied voices. At first he had tried to repress them but the counselors at the VA told him to share his feelings with Monique and that seemed to help. Gradually the flashbacks subsided but sometimes flared up again when he felt helpless.

Judy Goldman held on for dear life.

Why did I decide to go up in this thing? she thought as a steel cable with a hook pulled the parachute higher and higher.

"Mommy, mommy, look at ocean, isn't that cool?" Judy's five-year-old son Eric said as he sat next to her on the parachute ride at Coney Island. Across the blue expanse of water they could see ships on the horizon and white seagulls flying below.

"Yes, that's very cool," replied Judy trying to control her fear. The ride looked safe enough from the ground and Eric had pleaded for her to take him on it. She didn't get much time to spend with her son and had wanted to make the most of their time together.

When they reached the top the bench they were sitting on jerked to a halt and they began slowly swinging back and forth in the wind. She looked down and gasped.

Suddenly the hook released the parachute and they began to fall. They both screamed as several terrifying seconds passed before the parachute opened and they floated to the ground, guided by cables that ran alongside the canopy.

The young attendant, a pimply-faced kid with slicked back hair, unhitched the bar and Judy staggered down the ramp. She brushed back her hair and checked her necklace. She still had it. The gold heart on a chain was a gift from the man she was meeting at the amusement park today. They had only met once but Milos Kazantakis seemed like a nice man, a little old fashioned but she could handle that. They had been introduced through a friend of her brother's. Judy had planned on getting a baby sitter for Eric, but at the last minute the sitter couldn't make it. She hoped Milos would understand.

"Mommy, I want one of those," said Eric pulling at Judy's hand and pointing toward a booth with stuffed purple lions hanging from hooks. Five wooden posts protruded from a wall behind the booth. A pile of rings lay on the counter.

"How many posts do we have to get to win a prize," Judy asked the attendant, an old man with a cigar.

"Three out of five, five rings for a dollar."

Judy gave the man a dollar then helped Eric win a prize.

The old man smiled, reached below the counter and brought out a purple lion in a plastic bag. "Here's your lion, young man."

Judy took the bag and handed it to Eric then they walked down the boardwalk toward Nathan's to get a hot dog. Eric ran ahead of her and chased pigeons. He was a fearless kid, Judy thought. He was born when Judy was only sixteen. Eric's father was twenty and when he found out Judy was pregnant he left town. Now she was twenty-one and living with her mother who took care of Eric while she worked full-time a Bloomingdales in Manhattan. She had given up her teenage years for her son but was now ready to start dating again.

As she passed a mirror Judy glanced at her reflection. She liked the way her firm breasts filled out her sleeveless cotton top and her brown hair curled around her shoulders. Her legs were smooth and tan, without a trace of cellulite. "I've got a lot of living to do," she whispered.

Milos Kazantakis looked down the aisle of his furniture store and watched as a large black man with a sweat suit and tennis shoes walked quickly in his direction.

Milos slowly walked behind his desk at the end of the building and began looking through some invoices. He was a big man too and had developed strong muscles moving couches in the early days of his business shortly after he had arrived from Greece. However now he preferred to put some distance between himself and angry customers. When the man reached the desk Milos looked up.

"Can I help you?"

"I want my furniture back."

"And you are..."

"Mr. Johnson. I bought a couch and a TV from you six months ago and yesterday your boys came and picked them up."

"Just a minute," said Milos. He went to his file and thumbed through it until he produced an invoice and a record of payment form.

"It says here that you missed your May payment of $69.99."

"I was outa work for a while but I got the money now," said Mr. Johnson holding out three twenties and a ten.

"I'm sorry Mr. Johnson," said Milos, "but in your contract which you signed we have the right to repossess any item for which adequate payment is not made within the period of time specified in the contract. In your case that time period is within fifteen days of the first of the month."

"But I've got the money," said Mr. Johnson shaking his fist. "I've got your fuckin' money."

"No need to raise your voice Mr. Johnson," Milos said calmly. "Now I think you'd better leave." He picked up the phone and began dialing.

Mr. Johnson turned and began walking toward the door then turned around and pointed his finger at Milos. "I'm not forgetting this."

"Neither am I," said Milos as four burley furniture movers came down the stairs.

After work Milos changed his shirt and splashed on some aftershave. He had a date with Judy. She was a nice piece of ass, he thought. He would pick her up in a limo, take her to dinner and then try and get a little action.

Billy Washington dropped Mrs. Palmer off in Queens and then took Ocean Parkway to Coney Island. When he arrived he parked the limo in a taxi stand and walked across the boardwalk to Nathan's where he got a fried seafood bar. He checked his watch. Mr. Kazantakis was late.

He looked around. The crowd was beginning to get thicker. Across the table from him was a young woman leaning on the counter staring blankly at the parking lot with her fingers in her mouth. Three styrofoam takeout boxes were piled up in front of her. Below her under the counter was a young boy staring at a stuffed animal in a plastic bag.

Suddenly he heard his name.

"Billy? Is that you?"

He turned around. Milos Kazantakis was walking toward him. He shook Billy's hand and then walked over to the young woman and gave her a hug.

"Have you met Judy?" he said to Billy.

Billy looked at the girl and then looked at Milos. "I didn't know she was with you."

Judy held out her hand. "Pleased to meet you Billy."

Eric cowered in the corner.

"I hope you don't mind Eric coming, I couldn't find a babysitter," said Judy.

Milos scowled for a moment and then said, "That's OK." Then he squatted in front of Eric and said, "How would you like to sit up front with the driver."

Eric just stared

"Let's go," said Milos getting up.

They all got in the limo and drove to a diner near the amusement park. Billy waited in the limo while Eric napped in the front seat. After dinner they all took a drive down the beach. The sun was getting low and a cool breeze blew in from the north.

"Here, pull over here," said Milos directing Billy toward a deserted parking lot.

"Take this and buy the kid an ice cream cone," said Milos handing Billy a crumpled up dollar bill.

"Come on," Billy said to Eric who was just waking up from his nap wiping his eyes.

Something didn't feel right about the situation. "You mind if we get some ice cream?" Billy asked Judy.

"You go ahead. We just want to talk," said Judy.

Billy and Eric walked toward an ice cream stand about a quarter mile down the beach. When they got half way there Eric stopped.

"I want my lion."

"We'll get it later," said Billy taking Eric by the hand.

"I want it now. He'll get lonely without me."

"Okay, let's go back," said Billy taking Eric by the hand.

As they approached the limo from the rear it looked empty but as Billy walked around to the side he could see Milos in the back seat on top of Judy with his pants down.

"No, no," Judy cried.

Billy knocked on the window. Milos spun around and stared at Billy slack-jawed.

"Get the hell out of here," he yelled. "Can't you see I'm busy?"

"Mommy, mommy, are you all right," yelled Eric.

"Get the kid out of here," shouted Milos.

Billy jerked open the door and pulled Milos onto the pavement. He wasn't going to let it happen again. Not this time.

"What the fuck are you doing," Milos screamed as he tried to pull up his pants. Judy was crying.

"Mommy, mommy," screamed Eric.

Suddenly Billy started shaking as a hot wave of anger washed over him. When Milos got up Billy began pummeling him with his fists. Milos went back down and Judy began screaming, "Don't kill him."

Billy stepped back, took a deep breath and exhaled slowly. He walked to the other side of the car and opened the door to check on Judy.

"Are you okay," he asked.

"Yes, thanks," said Judy. "I don't know what would have happened if you hadn't come back when you did."

"Don't thank me, thank your son. He forgot his lion."

Eric jumped into his mother's arms and Billy got back into the limo.

Milos was just getting up on the side of the road. Aside from a couple scrapes from the pavement, he looked all right. "I just wanted a good time," he yelled as Billy drove off.

Billy dropped Judy and Eric off at their apartment then headed home. His head was clear and his hands were steady on the wheel. He felt better than he had in years.

The Cybernetic Possum

"How was your day," asked Monique when he walked into their small apartment. She looked beautiful, her belly full with their child. He threw his hat on a chair, crossed the room and gave her a kiss.

"It's finally over," he said.

Monique gave him a puzzled look. "What's over?"

Billy went to the refrigerator, took out a beer and sat down on the couch, patting the cushion next to him. "Have a seat, baby" he said, "and I'll tell you all about it."

Ramsey's World

Mike Ramsey was having one of those mornings again. His head was throbbing and he was going to be late for work. He had a vague memory of taking a cab home from the bar. The alarm hadn't gone off and the sun was peaking through his closed shades. He threw some water on his face and got dressed. He didn't want to be late again. This would be his third time in a month. He had been warned by his boss that he was seriously jeopardizing his job. He had a radio show to do. As he drove to the studio he decided to give *Alcoholics Anonymous* another try. OK, so maybe I have a drinking problem after all, he thought. Sure, I hate the meetings, they're attended by a bunch of losers, but I've got to try something.

When he got to the station he walked briskly down the short hall and into his studio. His engineer Alice was standing behind the glassed in control room.

Her gray hair was tied back in a bun and she was dressed in slacks and a Milwaukee Bucks tee-shirt. She had been working with Ramsey for ten years and was painfully aware of his late night binges. She looked up at him, smiled sadly then pointed to her watch.

"Nice of you to drop by," she said.

Ramsey smiled sheepishly and sat down. He put his coffee mug on the table, glanced at the morning schedule then fixed his gaze on the second hand of the clock on the wall. When the hand crossed the zenith of its arc Ramsey jabbed his finger at Alice. She flipped a switch and the studio was filled by the magnificent sound of bagpipes, the Massed Pipes and Drums of the Scottish Division playing, *Scotland the Brave.*

The Cybernetic Possum

Ramsey smiled and sat straighter in his chair as the music enveloped him with its heroic sound. After 15 seconds the bagpipes were replaced by the screaming electric guitar of Ted Nugent. At 30 seconds past the hour he waved to Alice and the music began to fade.

"Good morning Milwaukee, and welcome to *Ramsey's America*, the number one rated talk show that tells it like it is. We've got a great show for you today. We've got a young man who just returned from Iraq where he was awarded the Purple Heart for taking part in the liberation of Al-Fallujah from the terrorists. I'm so proud that he could be here today to share his story with us and I hope he will inspire you to support our troops in this time of national peril. Now some people have criticized me for being one sided so today we'll talk with the director of the Peace and Freedom Movement, Marvin Stein. Marvin thinks we're treating Al-Qaeda prisoners in Cuba inhumanely. We'll find out why in a minute after a word from the people who make this show possible."

Ramsey wound up like he was throwing a ball and jabbed his finger at Alice who cut to a commercial break. He poured himself another cup of coffee, reclined in his chair and began rubbing the back of his neck. Just then an image flashed in his mind. It was the memory of a dream he had the previous night, the drowning dream. It came to him in different forms on different nights-a memory from his childhood. In the dream he was thrashing around in the swimming pool after being tossed in by his father.

"Trust me," his father had said. "I wouldn't let you drown."

In the dream he was fighting for air then suddenly inhaled water and started choking.

"Daddy, help me," he cried

"You can't trust anyone. Save your self," his father replied.

He was going down, he was blacking out and his father wasn't going to rescue him.

Ramsey took a deep breath then noticed Alice banging on the glass in the control room. He snapped back to the present.

"Welcome back. On the telephone we've got Staff Sergeant Jose Ramirez from Texarkana, Arkansas with the 82nd Airborne who just returned from Iraq where he was awarded a Purple Heart. Welcome back Jose."

"Thank you sir, I'm glad to be on your show."

"We're proud to have you. I wonder if you could explain to the folks out there exactly what you and the other brave young men were doing over there."

"Well, Sir, currently we're helping train the Iraqis to take over some of the patrols in the Al Fallujah area. My platoon was involved in a firefight with the insurgents during the liberation last month and I caught a round in the shoulder."

"Well, we're all glad you weren't more seriously injured. How's it going?" asked Ramsey.

"The shoulder is healing up well, sir, and I'll be back with my unit pretty soon," said Sgt. Ramirez.

"That's just great. So what's going on over there? We hear reports in the news everyday about civilians dying and insurgents setting off roadside bombs that are killing our guys. I know the press is constantly looking for bad news to report but that can't be all that is going on can it?"

"No sir. In the Al Fallujah area we've rebuilt schools, restored electricity and we're working with the Navy's Seabees to put in a new water plant. We have civic action teams out immunizing children and performing dental work. I have many Iraqi friends and we're working together to turn this country around."

"Well, there you have it America. God bless you, Staff Sergeant Jose Ramirez," said Ramsey. "Our prayers go out to you and your family. Thank you for you service and for talking with America today."

After another commercial break Marvin Stein was on the phone.

"Good morning, Marvin," said Ramsey. "So let's cut right to the chase. What's all this yammering about the United States government torturing Al-Qaeda prisoners in Cuba? I think we all realize we're in a war with some pretty unsavory characters who will stop at nothing to destroy our civilization. I realize there are limits to what we can and can't do during interrogations but that issue has already been addressed by Attorney General Gonzales. Sure there are prison guards who break the law but they're punished. The United States government does not condone the use of torture".

"Well, actually it has been our policy for a long time now to torture prisoners, Mike. Our organization has documented reports…"

"Wait a minute," Ramsey broke in. "When you say you've got documented reports, where did you get your information? Did you turn that information over to military authorities so they could investigate it?"

"Well, we did and we've heard nothing back for …

"Of course you heard nothing back because you had nothing to begin with," said Ramsey, raising his voice.

"Actually we have testimony from former guards who said they took part in water boarding, which is a form of torture. In the procedure they put a towel over a prisoner's nose and mouth then pour water over it until he almost drowns. It's outlawed by the Geneva Convention that we have signed.

"Look sonny," said Ramsey, taking a deep breath, "There are a lot worse things they could do than to pour water on someone's head."

"I'm just saying that we're breaking international law by..."

"What are we supposed to do, serve them tea and crumpets and wait until they're ready to tell us what we want?" sneered Ramsey.

"Actually the information we get from torture is rarely considered reliable because…"

"Just a minute here," demanded Ramsey. "Let's get something straight. The United States does not torture prisoners, period end of discussion. The justice department has investigated and Attorney General Gonzales has issued a report that categorically denies that charge."

"They just redefined the word torture to include what would normally…"

"All right, I've heard enough. You and your peacenik friends can all go and sit in a circle somewhere and join hands and sing songs and let people who really care about this country do their jobs. We've got to go to a commercial break and when we come back we'll talk to school kids at Holy Redeemer School in Roselawn, Indiana who have taken up a collection to buy Bibles for kids in the only Christian school in Baghdad."

After the show Mike Ramsey had a few drinks at the Downtown Bar then grabbed a cab to the airport. He caught a late night flight to New York City where he was giving a speech to the Society of Christian Journalists.

It was after midnight at John F. Kennedy International Airport in New York and passenger traffic had slowed to a trickle.

Special Agent Joseph Cutler was bored. He sat at his desk and twisted a rubber band around his index finger. When his finger began to turn white he let go and watched the rubber band spin off and fly across the room. He picked it off the rug then shot it at the computer monitor on his desk. The monitor displayed a list of names: Owen Jennings, Alex Jenson, William Keene, Thomas Knotts, William Lamb, Jerry Martin, Daniel McDonald, Michael Ramsey, Fredrick Beemis, John Scarborough…that were on a watch list. Some of the names came from Scotland Yard, some from the CIA, and the rest from a smattering of other intelligence agencies like the Russian FSB, and Britain's M5.

Cutler had just returned from a three-month deployment to Afghanistan where he was working as a Clandestine Service Operations Officer in charge of training the Afghan Army's intelligence units in interrogation techniques.

He glanced up at the one-way glass window in front of him and saw the Homeland Security team screening luggage on the other side.

He yawned and took another swig of coffee. He'd been smoking more than he wanted and had been feeling like a caged animal ever since he returned to the states.

"We're going to give you a little break and assign you to airport security," his boss had told him. "We want you to decompress for a while but we can't spare the personnel so we gave you a cushy post."

"How about an expense paid trip to Cancun?" asked Cutler.

"No can do," said his boss a thin woman with short brown hair and a no-nonsense attitude.

"Right."

Cutler took a last swig of coffee, crumpled up the paper cup and threw it over his head looping it into the wastebasket in the corner.

Suddenly there was a commotion on the security monitor. A man was waving his hands in the air and three security guards were moving him back from the screening portal.

Cutler flipped on the speaker.

"I'm gonna be late, don't you understand?" the man was saying in a loud voice.

"Please sir," said a heavy security guard who looked like a retired grocer. "Just step this way for a moment."

"What's going on here?" demanded the passenger.

Cutler put on his blazer, went outside and flashed his badge.

"Let's go into another room and talk."

They went inside a small room which contained a table and some chairs.

"Have a seat." he said. The big man with a gray suit and an American flag pin on the lapel looked at the table and the chair, hesitated for a moment then sat down.

Agent Cutler sat opposite him and the two HS guards stood on either side. Suddenly there was a knock on the door. One of the guards opened it and went outside.

"Could we see some identification?" asked Cutler.

"Wait a minute here," the passenger said. "Don't you recognize me? I'm Mike Ramsey, nationally syndicated host of *Ramsey's America*."

Agent Cutler looked at the guard who returned a blank stare. The other guard returned and whispered something in Cutler's ear. He turned to Ramsey.

"I'm sorry sir, but I'd really like to see some identification."

Ramsey produced his driver's license. Cutler studied it then handed it back.

"Jesus, you act like I'm gonna blow up the plane or something," said Ramsey.

"Mister Ramsey," Cutler said shaking his head in amazement. "You just said the wrong thing."

"Hey, I didn't say I *was* going to blow up the plane. I'm really going to deliver a speech to the Society of Christian Journalists."

Cutler got up. "I'm placing you under arrest sir." He nodded to the two HS guards who stepped forward on either side of him.

"Stand up and place your hands behind your back, sir."

Ramsey stared in disbelief. The guards grabbed his arms but he resisted until they slammed him to the table and cuffed him.

"What are you arresting me for?"

"Making verbal threats regarding explosive materials, resisting arrest, and suspicion of terrorist activities," said Cutler. He turned to the guards. "Take him downtown."

"What? What are you doing? You can't do this to me. This is America. I've got rights. I demand to speak to a lawyer," protested Ramsey.

"As a terrorist suspect you have no rights," said Cutler.

The guards said nothing more and bundled Ramsey out a side door and onto the tarmac where a black unmarked SUV was waiting. They put him in the back seat which was separated from the front by a metal grate and drove away amidst the loud whine of jet engines and the pungent smell of jet fuel.

"Wise ass," said Cutler, beneath his breath. "You don't screw with the United States government."

The HS men drove north toward the lighted skyscrapers of New York City, across the Brooklyn Bridge then into the receiving area of the Metropolitan Correctional Center in lower Manhattan. They took his belt and shoes and put him in a cell with a toilet and a metal table.

New York City Police Commissioner Randall Mendez was working late in his office. He had taken a break and was staring out of the window at the lights of the city.

They're down there somewhere, he thought. Maybe they're in some warehouse near the East River putting it together right now. How long do we have? Maybe twelve hours, maybe twenty-four? There's no way of telling.

Suddenly the phone rang.

He picked up the receiver. "Mendez here."

"I think we've got one of them." It was the voice of agent Cutler.

Mendez leaned forward. "Are you sure?"

"We're running the checks now. Same name, same description. We think he's IRA. Mike Ramsey. We were interrogating him and he joked about having a bomb- very uncooperative. You want us to wait until morning to finish questioning him?"

"No," snapped Mendez. "We don't have the time. Get him softened up first. Let's begin phase one tonight. Get him transferred into federal custody."

"Right, talk to you in the morning."

Mendez smiled as he hung up the phone. He wondered if it could be that easy. Like the Roch killings in 2001 when one of his patrol officers pulled over a car with a defective taillight and found a corpse in the trunk. He got captain for that. Now he was running for the US House of Representatives from the Bronx and this just drops in his lap. He thought it must be fate.

Ramsey was only in the holding tank for about a half hour when they moved him to another cell, a place of absolute darkness. Why me, he wondered? What did I do? It's a mistake, a horrible mistake. He waited for someone to open the door but no one came.

"Hey," he yelled. "Hey, where's the light switch." He was still handcuffed but managed to turn around and begin feeling the wall. He slid his hands along its' smooth surface until he got to a long vertical shaft where the door was then moved across the door until he got to a corner. He crouched down. The only sound he heard was the thumping of his heart and the only thing he smelled was his own strong body odor. He grimaced in pain as the metal bracelets cut into his wrists. He shifted his position and tried to be perfectly still. The pain subsided.

'Hey, I want to talk to my lawyer. Hey, hey," he shouted again but there was no response.

Suddenly he felt a pain in his chest and began to gasp. I'm going to die. He crumpled forward and hit his head on the wall. The pain in his chest subsided replaced by throbbing in his temples. Maybe I'm not having a heart attack. Maybe it's just gas. He began gasping for air then realized he was hyperventilating and tried to relax. He took a couple deep breaths and exhaled slowly. There, that's better.

He was thirsty now, very thirsty and his tongue began sticking to his upper palate. He tied not to think about it. He dozed off and woke up with a start. How long have I been sleeping? The thirst had gone away but now he had to urinate.

He banged on the door and called out, "Hey, hey, I've gotta take a piss." No response, just darkness and the foul smell of his own body. He held it for as long as he could then let it go and felt the moist warmth spreading out around his scrotum then down his inner thigh. How long have I been here, four or five hours? He closed his eyes and tried to relax. Inside of his head specks of light condensed into pulsating red and white flashes followed by green and purple waves like an incoming tide. Later the shapes developed human forms and faces. There were the images of the guards and Cutler and dark shadows that flew around like phantoms. Next came the bits and pieces of random memories that replayed in no particular sequence: the face of Alice, the lights of New York City as he was landing, his ex-wife, the jukebox at the bar, roses at his mother's funeral. The images were flashing through his head which still ached from the fall.

Suddenly the door swung open and the cell was flooded with light. Ramsey shielded his eyes. Two guards pulled him to his feet and led him down a white hall to small room with a gray desk and two chairs. On one wall there was a mirror. He glanced at his reflection and saw an old man with a stain on his pants. They sat him on a chair, unlocked his handcuffs and left. Ramsey held his hands up in front of his face.

There was a red gash in the thin skin on the inside of each wrist and his shoulders ached. He felt a little faint and laid his head on the desk.

He heard the door open and Ramsey looked up. A deeply suntanned man with a military crew cut came in bearing a cup of coffee. It was the same man who had arrested him. He had a silver badge, a nametag which read "Cutler" and a small folder. He put the coffee on the table.

"Coffee?" he said.

Ramsey leaned back.

"Yeah, thanks."

"Sorry about the accommodations. My name is agent Cutler. I'm from the Department of Homeland security." They shook hands.

"I've got a few questions to ask you."

"Shoot pal," said Ramsey taking a sip of coffee.

"Let's see," said Cutler, taking out the sheet. "So you're Michael Ramsey from Milwaukee, Wisconsin.

Cutler opened the folder and took out a printed piece of paper and some photographs.

Ramsey took another sip of coffee and burned his tongue.

Cutler handed Ramsey a black and white picture of a woman with dark short cropped hair and wire rimmed glasses.

"Have you ever seen her before?"

The picture blurred and Ramsey tried to focus.

"Nope never have."

Cutler gave him another picture, this time of a man with a beard and the woman talking at a luncheon. "Take another look," he said.

Ramsey looked at the picture. "I meet a lot of people at conferences. I don't remember her. What's this about? What do you want to know?"

"Take another look," said Cutler.

What did he want? Maybe he'd seen her at the Friends of Ireland dinner he was at last year. She looked sort of familiar.

"I don't know who she is. Just someone I was talking with."

"You've gotta do better than that," said Cutler, raising his voice. "Let's get this over with. Just tell us what you know"

"I wish I could tell you something."

"Mr. Ramsey, you're making this very difficult for yourself. You're forcing me to do something I don't want to do."

"Fuck you Cutler," Ramsey shouted. "I'm an American citizen. You can't keep me caged up like an animal without any charge. I don't know what's going on here but I'm gonna expose your little operation on my radio show and you're going to be very, very sorry you ever crossed me."

"No, fuck you Ramsey," said Cutler. "We've got a very serious situation here and you're gonna give me some answers. Culter got up and summoned the guards. "Take him away."

Later that afternoon Cutler got a call from Police Commissioner Mendez.

"It looks like we've got our man," said Mendez. "We caught him trying to climb up a pylon of the Brooklyn Bridge with a satchel of explosives."

"That's great," said Cutler running his fingers through his hair. "I guess that means we've got a little problem here."

"What kind of problem?"

"Our people missed something. Apparently Ramsey really does have his own radio show in Milwaukee. I hate to say this but we've got the wrong Mike Ramsey. Now he wants to make trouble for us."

"How the hell did that happen?" exploded Mendez.

"You gave the orders to begin interrogation," said Cutler.

Mendez was quite for a while. "These things happen every now and then," he said in a robotic monotone. "See what you can do to convince him that he really doesn't want to cause us any problems." He hung up.

Ramsey was led back to his cell, stripped of his clothes and his hands were cuffed behind him. Suddenly the vents began pouring cold air into the cell and he began to shiver. He retreated to a corner of his cell and lay down on the floor to get out of the line of the frigid blast. As he lay there shivering a sprinkler head mounted on the ceiling began spraying him with water. He began shaking violently. Soon his body grew numb and he lost consciousness.

He wasn't sure how long he lay there. The door silently opened and the guards woke him up with smelling salts.

"Here," one of them said and threw Ramsey an orange jumpsuit. They watched him get dressed and took him back to the interrogation room.

When Cutler came back in he had a bottle of scotch and a shot glass with him. He laid them on the table.

"Have a drink," he said. "You deserve one."

Cutler's hands were shaking so badly that he spilled the scotch all over the table.

"Here, let me do it," said Cutler. He poured Ramsey a shot.

"Why are you doing this?" said Ramsey, his teeth still chattering.

"Hey, I just thought you needed a drink, bottoms up!"

Ramsey took a sip. It was good whisky and it went down easy.

"Have another one."

He had a couple more and stopped shivering.

Cutler threw the picture of the woman on the table. "What's her name?"

"I dunno."

"Have another drink."

"I've had enough."

Ramsey suddenly slumped forward. The two guards came in and one of them raised Ramsey's head while the other forced Ramsey's jaws open and began dumping the scotch down his throat.

Suddenly Ramsey began choking and vomited. He couldn't get his breath. "Help me," he cried.

"Help yourself," said Cutler. "Help yourself."

He was going down, he was losing consciousness. A picture of his father flashed into his mind. He vomited again and finally got a breath.

"OK, OK, the woman, the woman, was Mary Conners," sobbed Ramsey wiping the snot from his face. " She was....she was an IRA, no she was the wife of Jimmy Conners...an IRA sympathizer...no he was really a bomb maker...she wanted me to put her on my show...no she wanted me to smuggle some guns into the country." He looked up at Cutler. "Is that what you want? I can tell you more."

"That'll do," said Cutler. "Get him cleaned up."

"But what was this all about?" whined Ramsey. He saw room was spinning.

Cutler left without replying. The guards gave Ramsey his clothes and a piece of bread. It was Sunday evening.

Monday morning Ramsey failed to show up for work and the network put on a rerun. His producer found out he missed the Christian Broadcaster's meeting and was concerned. On Wednesday an anonymous caller said that he saw Ramsey drunk in a bar Friday night. He was fired *in absentia.*

The C-130 banked and began a steep descent toward an arid coastline. The sunlight woke Ramsey and he opened his eyes. He had the worst hangover of his life. His head was pounding and his tongue felt like a dried out sock. He had no idea where he was. His hands and feet were shacked but as the plane descended he managed to crane his neck around to catch a glimpse out the window. All he could see was white sand. As the plane landed a chill ran through Ramsey's body. In an oasis next to the field was a herd of camels tended to by a man in a long white robe.

Cab Stories-Buck's Tavern

I'm sitting in my cab at the Concourse Hotel one night reading the newspaper when I get a call for Buck's Tavern.

I pull up in front of the bar which has a large picture window and honk twice. I wait a couple minutes and am about to go in when a blond woman sticks her head out the door and holds up her index finger.

"She'll be out in a minute," she calls out, smiling.

Cab driver intuition tells me that my passenger is probably sitting at the bar staring glassy eyed at a jar of pickled eggs with a full shot of whisky in front of her. The bartender had probably called the cab and is eager to get rid of her before she either passes out of loses her lunch on the floor.

My fears are confirmed moments later when the bartender comes out partially supporting a heavy set woman with dark curly hair wearing designer jeans and spiked heels. Reluctantly I reach behind me to push open the door.

Instead the bartender takes her customer around the front of the cab, opens the passenger door and lowers her into the seat.

"Take good care of my friend," she says with a broad smile. She closes the door, waves good-bye and then runs back inside.

The woman suddenly turns toward me with a surprised look like she realizes for the first time that she's in a cab. She lunges forward, throws her arms around my shoulders and pins me against the window.

"Where are we going honey?" she asks. She smells like cigarettes and alcohol with a hint of cheap perfume.

"That's what I was going to ask you," I say. "Why don't I take you home?"

Her eyes light up. "Yeah, let's go over to my place."

I manage to loosen her grip on my neck long enough to ease her over to the other side of the seat and then get her address.

I throw the hook and pull away from the curb. "Just don't throw up in my cab," I say. "If you feel like throwing up tell me and I'll stop the cab, O.K?"

She says OK and we drive to her apartment. When we get there I stop the meter at $1.70. She fumbles around in her purse, gives me three crumpled up dollar bills and tells me to keep the change.

"How about a goodnight kiss?" she says, getting up on her knees and pinning me against the door again. What the hell, I think. Maybe if I give her friendly little kiss I'll be rid of her. Besides, I have no other choice.

I kiss her quickly and say, "OK, have a nice night." I'm kidding myself. She grabs my head and gives me a long hard kiss.

"I don't think we should be doing this," I say. She pays no attention to me. I slide down low so nobody will see and we kiss a while longer. Finally I push her away and grab a breath of fresh air.

"OK, that's enough. I'll help you to the door." I go around to the passenger side and open the door. She's a bit wobbly so I take her arm and we walk up a short path to her front door.

"Will you be OK?" I ask as she fumbles with her key chain.

"Just a minute honey," she says. She puts a key into the lock and jiggles it around but it won't turn. Technically I had completed my job. I transported her to her destination and had been paid. But now I'm feeling a tender spot in my heart for her and feel obliged to make sure she gets into her apartment safely.

I turn around and check to see if anyone is watching. "This isn't what it appears to be," I murmur to myself.

"Here, let me try it," I say and pull the key from the lock. I try another key and turn the knob. She squeals with delight.

"Come on in honey," she says pushing open the door.

"Oh, no thanks, I've got another call," I lie as two cats dart through my legs out into the yard.

"My babies," she cries. "Help me get my babies."

We round up her cats and get them back inside. I wish her a good night and head back to my cab.

"Number 27, where are you?" the dispatcher asks.

"Twenty-seven…I just dropped my fare."

"Twenty-seven…go to the Crystal Corner. MPD called it in. Your passenger is intoxicated."

"Ten-four…what's new?" I reply. It was going to be a long night.

Wars Never End

I'm cruising down East Wash in my cab one Saturday night when I get a call for the Pizza Hut. I pull up and this tall dude with a beard and a floppy hat gets in smelling of booze.

"I figured it was better to call a cab than get another ticket for DWI ya know Cap'n?" he says.

Right away I recognized him as the Vietnam veteran I'd taken bar hopping a few weeks earlier.

"Yeah, good idea," I say. "Where are you going?"

"Dayton Street."

"Any particular address?"

"1141."

"Thanks."

I flip on the meter and turn around in the parking lot.

"I better not get caught DWI again," he says. "Judge gave me six-months last time. I'm gonna watch Willie on TV tonight. They really fucked him up Cap'n– took all his money. Government fucked him over just like they fucked me over." I don't know who Willie is but decide not to ask.

We pull out onto the Avenue and begin heading up-town.

"Fucked me up in 'Nam," he says. "Made me get down on my hands and knees, asked me if wanted a bowl of rice and I said 'sure'. Made me crawl man, like I was some kind of animal."

He's quiet for a while then when we cross First and the Avenue I look in my rear-view mirror and see him take a flask from his pocket, screw off the cap and take a swig.

"Hey man," I say. "Don't drink that shit in here. I can't have an open bottle of booze in the cab. I could lose my license."

The Cybernetic Possum

"OK, Cap'n–sorry," he says and puts the bottle back .
"Army fucked me over seventeen-years ago."
"That's a long time ago," I say.
"Not long enough Cap'n. Not long enough."

Rocky Mountain High

It was toward the end of July in 1975 when tiny squares of gelatin laced with LSD began showing up in the little Colorado mountain town of Oak Creek.

The town, with a population of 849, is located at the bottom of a dip in state highway 131 in the semi-arid Yampa River valley of north central Colorado. The former coal mining town had recently staked its hopes for revival on the construction of a nearby ski resort. Workers had poured into the town but construction was halted after a snag in financing. Many of the workers who remained were still surviving on welfare checks and odd jobs, savoring the laid back Rocky Mountain lifestyle.

I was spending a couple weeks visiting a friend there and had staked out a couch at the "crash house" on the hill in exchange for two bags of groceries. I had heard that a woman from California named Maria had brought some acid into town. I didn't know where she was but when I saw a beautiful, dark haired girl with silver rings on her wrists and ankles walking barefoot down the main street with a bunch of ragged hippies, I knew I had found my connection.

I went up to her and bought a hit of window pane for two dollars. I had done acid a couple times in the past with varying results but felt fairly confident that the current environment increased the odds of having a good trip.

After Maria and her band moved on down the street I licked the acid off a piece of tin foil then stood there bracing for the drug's onset. It didn't take long. Everything around me slowly began to vibrate. Then I heard a low hum followed by the appearance of a pink halo around things. The acid slowly crept up my spine then hit my brain like eggs in a skillet. For a moment I couldn't move. Slowly I began walking toward the Colorado Bar where I found a barstool in a corner next to a guy with a cowboy hat and mirror sunglasses. I ordered a beer and tried to relax. When the cowboy turned to face me I was startled to see the reflection of a fish head.

"Just stay cool and ride it out," the cowboy said in a soothing tone. "I find it's best to sit here with a Budweiser and kinda get adjusted."

"Yeeeeehhhh, thaaat's alllllll riiiiiiiight," replied the fish head.

I guzzled down the beer and left.

I wandered up a hill to the edge of town where there was a junkyard of abandoned cars and refrigerators surrounded by a small log-cut fence then ambled through the gateless entrance. Off in the distance was a mountain on the other side of a field of cattails. I looked again. It didn't have a snow capped peak and was covered with trees except for a bare spot on the top. Maybe it's just a high hill…or is it? I had to find out. I drew a bead across the field and up the side of the mountain.

I ran to the other side of the corral, vaulted over the rail fence and headed down into the cattails. I jumped over some low hanging barbed wire in the knick of time, crossed a shallow stream and began my ascent. There was no trail, so I climbed straight up grasping at bunches of grasses and roots.

When I reached the summit I looked down and saw Oak Creek on one side of the mountain and the neighboring town of Phippsburg on the other. A train was passing between the towns and I could actually hear the clacking of the wheels on the tracks. Lying on the ground next to me was a rusty communication tower. Overhead a few dark cumulus clouds slowly drifted by.

As I was watching the clouds I noticed some hawks circling overhead. As they swooped closer to me they turned their heads and looked as if to say, what is this human doing on our mountain? I could see their sharp beaks and hear their cries. I had read several books by Carlos Castaneda about a Yaqui Indian sorcerer named Don Juan who knew how to talk with spirits through animals. I thought that I could do the same.

I raised my fist for a perch and called to the hawks, "Come and let us speak." This only seemed to infuriate the winged spirits as they swooped closer toward me. Suddenly a bolt of electricity shot through my body. I looked down and saw smoke coming from the ground. At first I thought I was hallucinating. But the electric shock? Where did that come from? Holy shit… I've been struck by lightening…tower attracted electrical charge… nearly fried… mountain gods want me down.

Just as I had run straight up the mountain so I ran straight down crashing through thick brush as the hawks screamed and swooped above, their talons outstretched. I picked up a stout branch to beat them off should they decide to dive down for the kill. I was about two-thirds of the way down when I started thinking. Here I am on heavy drugs running recklessly down a steep mountain. Only one such as my self with superhuman powers could even attempt such a feat. Suddenly my legs buckled and I went down. I tumbled then tried to regain my balance only to fall again.

When I reached the bottom I picked myself up. The hawks were gone. I had only sustained a few scrapes but had no idea where I was. I followed a little brook which flowed through a green pasture until I saw some cattle on the other side. A cow and her calf were heading downstream but the calf was limping. A wave of guilt washed over me. My rampaging through the brush must have frightened it. I had injured a mother's baby. My eyes filled with tears as I followed the path until it veered off toward the highway.

When I reached the road I wandered back and forth trying to decide which way to go. One way was to Oak Creek and the other way was to Phippsburg. There was a ranch about 200 yards to my left but I wasn't about to knock on the door and ask for directions. Not after trespassing on their land and possibly injuring their cattle. The narrow two-lane road disappeared around a hill to my right and the only highway marking was a speed limit sign shot full of holes. I took the road to my right figuring I'd have an even chance of ending up in the right place. My gamble paid off.

I walked past the baseball diamond on the outskirts of town then down the main street toward the café. An occasional pick-up truck rolled by but paid me no mind. Everything looked pretty normal—no pulsating buildings or dancing telephone poles. I decided to go into the café to get something to eat. After my near-fatal brush with death I was very hungry.

As soon as I walked in I felt out of place. There were tables to be sat at and chairs to be sat on. There was a waitress to talk to and a cash register to collect my money, all social constructs—parts of the real world that now seemed alien.

There were no other customers. I walked to a table and sat down. There that wasn't very difficult. I may be able to pull this off after all. The waitress came out of the kitchen. She was an older woman with grey hair, possibly a long time Oak Creek resident. I knew I'd have to mind my manners. She brought me a menu and I remembered to say "Thank you." But when tried to read it the lines of print ran together. I couldn't differentiate "beverages" from "deserts" or "lunch" from "dinner."

I ended up ordering a piece of apple pie and coffee. When the waitress brought my pie I stared at it for several minutes. Should I eat it with my hands or use the fork? While I was grappling with this dilemma the waitress returned with my coffee presenting me with another problem. Should I drink the coffee first or eat the pie? I remembered that I took cream and sugar with my coffee, so there was no problem with that. There was even a silver pitcher of cream on the table and a glass container of sugar with a pour spout.

I'd better do something...don't want to draw attention to myself. I picked up my fork, made the first cut into the pointed end of the pie and raised it to my mouth. Plop! It fell onto the table. I decided to try the coffee then work my way up to the harder stuff.

While I was struggling with my food, three hippies walked in and sat at the table next to me. I looked up from my task and nodded. There were two guys and a girl. One of the guys wore a red scarf around his neck and a floppy leather hat with a feather sticking out of it. The other one had a black untrimmed beard and silver wire-rimmed glasses. The young woman had a purple headband tied around her long blond hair. She wore a green ankle-length granny dress and hiking books. I had never seen them in town before. I smiled and they smiled back.

I turned my attention back to the dropped piece of pie lying on the table cloth. I scooped it up with my hands then shoved it into my mouth. It tasted wonderful. I washed it down with some coffee then scraped the rest of the pie off the table with a spoon. I heard snatches of conversation coming from the booth next to me. It sounded like they were talking about some land they were thinking of buying. That gave me an opening.

"You folks gonna buy some land around here?"

The guy with the beard slowly rolled his eyes in my direction.

"Well, we was lookin' at some," he said slowly. "Don't know if we're gonna buy it. Growin' season's awful short up here."

"Yeah," I said.

The waitress poured me more coffee. I could feel the synapses in my brain slowly resume firing in a semi normal pattern. Growing season... sure would be hard to get any crops going... snow 'til late

May ...comes back at the end of September...only two or three months of decent farming conditions.

"You people into farming?" I asked.

The guy with the beard looked at the guy with the hat and both of them looked at the young woman with the bandana. She turned around and said, "We're scouting out some land for the people."

I nodded. The people... sounds like she thinks their people were special...many Indian tribal names translated into English mean "the people." They looked like they were some kind of white, migratory tribesmen...maybe the Rainbow Tribe... a communal band of roving mountain hippies...into peyote rituals, LSD, mysticism and white witchcraft.

"Are you from the Rainbow People?" I asked.

They all smiled and nodded.

"How's the acid."

Perty decent," said the guy with the hat.

The only sign he was tripping was a twinkle in his the eyes and a quiet sort of camaraderie with the others who I assumed were also tripping. I smiled again and raised my coffee cup in a toast.

After I finished the rest of my pie and coffee I paid my bill and went outside where I was blinded by sunlight. I tried to refocus my eyes without much success then walked back to the Colorado Bar where I ordered a beer. I went into a small room off the main bar and tried playing pool with a tall, blond haired construction worker named Gus. We played eight-ball and he broke but didn't get anything in. I grabbed a cue, chalked up then bent down to shoot but missed. The table was changing from a rectangle to a trapezoid. Gus was laughing and his body was becoming elongated like Plastic Man.

"God damn it Gus," I yelled. "Stop contorting your body like that. How the hell am I supposed to make a shot?"

I gave up trying to shoot pool when my buddy Reilly whom I was visiting walked it. We had a couple more beers and I told him about my adventures on the mountain. Later we took a drive to the hot springs outside of nearby Steamboat Springs. When we got there it was getting dark and a full moon was rising. We shimmied down the steep bank and stripped down leaving our clothes on the rocks. Reilly brought out a bottle of wine and we soaked in the springs until the fireflies came out and the moon cast a pale glow on the tall spruce trees standing next to the stream as it slowly licked its way down the mountainside.

Poems

The Cybernetic Possum

While driving to the store one night
to buy a present for my sweet
I saw what looked to me to be
a possum sitting in the street.

His two front legs were standing
but his rear ones seemed to sit
and as I drove on past him
it appeared that he'd been hit.

I clenched my teeth in silence
and sucked my stomach in
because I felt that when I passed
it was an awful sin.

For what good are we as humans
if it's not in our moral code
to help a half-smashed possum
just a'sittin' in the road.

The thought it would not leave me
as I traveled to the store.
I knew that poor old possum
was feeling mighty sore.

I vowed before I drove on back
that I would spend some bread
to buy a possum basket
and hope he wasn't dead.

I bought a yellow basket
and hoped it wasn't too late
to save my friend the possum
from some destructive fate.

With two strong legs I'd raise him
and feed him possum meals
and if his back legs would not walk
I'd build him possum wheels.

What a strange sight to behold.
What a friendship that would blossom.
When I took him on a walk they'd say,
"Here comes the cybernetic possum."

The Cybernetic Possum

But alas, the road was barren
as I drove slowly through the night
and I searched at every roadside bend
with my headlights set at bright.

I know to some this may sound odd
and I do not mean to scoff
but I should have stopped my car and helped
instead of driving off.

A Post Vietnam Memorial Day

The guns were fired.
A wreath was laid.
A widow cried.
A speech was made.

Some poor bastard
laid out in a tomb.
They said he died for his country,
but he died too soon.

If they'd have told him what
he was really fighting for
he'd have stayed at home,
he'd have locked his door.

He'd have raised his kids
and made love to his wife.
He'd have helped his neighbors.
He'd have had a good life.

Instead he died for lies
too long on the shelf.
He died fightin' communism
which died by itself.

The Cybernetic Possum

He died for Halliburton,
He died for Lockheed.
He died for power.
He died for greed.

And when this veterans'
time has passed
they can bury me face down
so corporations can kiss my ass.

An Inside Job

She said the hotel must have known,
there were many rapes before.
The bellman had just left the room
when he came rushing through the door.

He pushed her to the rug
and put a blindfold over her eyes,
stuck a gun into her throat
and raped her as she cried.

Six years ago it happened,
now when her head begins to throb
she feels the gun down in her throat.
It was an inside job.

Bad Poetry

Bad poetry is what I'm writing,
but I must write it now.
I know not what I'm writing,
or why or what or how.

All I know is I must write it,
because the hour is late
and I've got to lay my pen aside,
because I've got a date.

And after having written it,
I look back upon my pad
and reading what I've written
it's really not that bad.

Brain Dead

Brain dead at the age of 47
he could frequently be found staring
at a blank page of paper.
We knew not what thoughts might be racing
through his brain but
if there were any
they didn't show up on the monitor.
Yet when we tried to pry the notebook
from his hands he resisted.
The doctors thought it best to let him
keep it because
there had been documented cases of
spontaneous remissions from such conditions, although
they are rare in the literature of neuroscience.

Casualty of the Feminist Revolution

He's a casualty of the feminist revolution,
trying to define his constitution,
breaking every resolution
he made in earlier days.

Desperately searching for a solution,
to be granted some measure of absolution
he sits in utter confusion,
hoping for better days.

Dog Shit

Dog shit lying on the grass,
ain't you got no sense of class?
Can't you see the lawn is growing?
Go somewhere else so I can start mowing!

Early Spring

Hey you friggin' stubby sprout
what the hell are you doing out?

Hey you naked jogger runnin' past
don't you know you'll freeze your ass?

And you, you stupid singin' bird
I don't believe what I just heard.

'Cuz I'm the spirit of winter ya know,
and I'll freeze you stiff before I go.

Farewell to Hardies

I looked in the mirror the other day,
blinked my eyes then turned away
because as the winter winds were blowing
the fat around my waist kept growing.

A pizza here, a cookie there
to keep me warm, it sounded fair.
Some M&M's while on the go
to help me concentrate you know.

A pound of two of weight each month
didn't seem like such a bunch
until the time of spring arrived
with a glutinous mass of fat archived.

So now it's time to say good-bye
to Hardies clubs and curly French fries
and day-old doughnuts grabbed on the run.
With this heavy load of guilt they are no fun.

Those days of gastronomic delight are past
in hopes the latest regimen will last
and soon self-discipline will be the winner
so that by July I'll be ten pounds thinner.

Hacking It

You asked me how I did today
so sit back down and let me say;
two no-loads and twenty-five trips,
booked 112 dollars and 30 in tips.

A full shift worked in a long snow shower,
that comes down to ten dollars per hour.
Before I checked in I saw a two-car wreck,
got a kink in my back and a sore neck.

Picked up a masseuse at *This is Heaven,*
the fare was $6.90 and she gave me seven.
While doing a delivery picked up a flag,
got six bucks out of him but I won't brag
because there will be another day
when I know that things won't go my way.

Huge Burrito

Had a huge burrito at the Little Village
and soon my intestines it began to pillage.
The gas backed up all the way to my heart
then turned around and came out as a fart.

The wall paper peeled and my cat fell dead,
my plants all wilted when I went to bed.
When I got up in the middle of the night
the bedroom blew up when I turned on the light.

The blast smashed me like a big mosquito
and now I'm up in heaven craving another burrito.

March First

Thank God, it's here at last.
The month of February has finally past.
Now spring begins its' slow transition
as I improve my disposition.

Long dormant brain cells begin to churn
and soon the desire will begin to burn
for open roads and far off lands—
grist for idle minds and idle hands.

Ozone Hole

The ozone hole is gonna kill us.
It's Mother Nature's time to bill us,
for debts that have become past due.
It's judgment day for me and you.

The Thin Blue Line

The veneer of racial harmony
had for years been wearing thin
but then one day on the streets of LA
came a black man named Rodney King.
The dude was wired with PCP
or so the LA cops thought,
so they beat him to the ground with clubs,
it was the way they were taught.
But a guy in his pad overlooking the scene
got it all on his VCR.
The press was invited as the cops were indicted
and Rodney healed his scars.
Fourteen months later the tables were turned
as the jury let the cops walk.
The rifles were loaded, the ghetto exploded
and nobody wanted to talk.
Flames licked the sky as fifty people would die
and the Guard put a lid on the city.
Burned out buildings remained,
the neighborhood was shamed
and even Rodney would say, it ain't pretty.
At a terrible cost everyone lost
and nobody claimed being a winner.
After 3,000 arrests and the ghetto a mess,
the thin blue line just got thinner.

Tripping in My Dreams

I woke this morning sore and tired
because all night long my brain was wired,
into a paranoid plot where I expired.
I was tripping in my dreams.

Although I woke up feeling guilty
from the fantasy I built within me;
I swore off acid 'cuz it nearly kilt me,
I was tripping in my dreams.

New brain chemistry not withstanding,
old patterns lost were now rebranding.
Despite my frantic reprimanding,
I was tripping in my dreams.

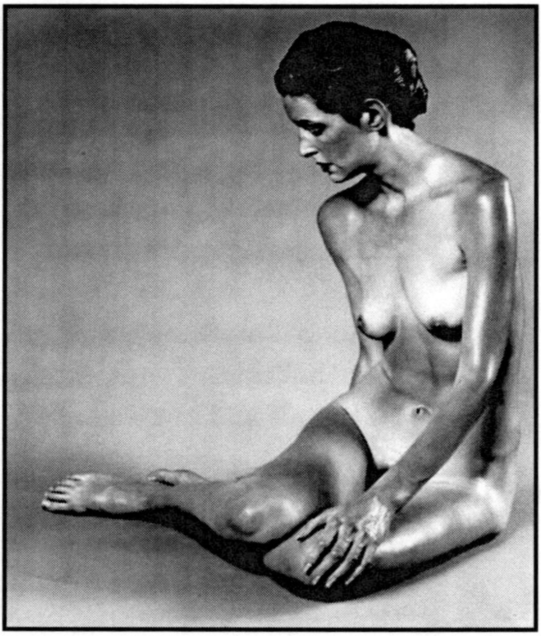

John Louis De Andrea
Untitled Bronze #1 1984 Oil on Bronze

Chazen Museum of Art, University of Wisconsin-Madison,
Elvehjem Endowment Fund & Harry and Margaret P. Glicksman
Endowment Fund purchase, 1985.90

Hey Baby!

Ode to "Untitled Bronze #1"

Hey baby,
whatcha doin' there
sittin' all alone.
I couldn't help but notice you
cuz all your clothes are gone.

I really dig your body
from your fingers to your toes
and I can tell that you're a lady,
a fact the clearly shows.

Now I'm getting kind of lonely
so I'll stay real near
and when the museum closes
maybe we can have a beer.

I'll have you back Sunday morning
and sneak through the back door,
so you can perform your still life
just staring at the floor.

TV Clicker

TV clicker...I am addicted to you.
I love how your slim rectangular frame
fits snugly in the palm of my eager hand.
I thrill to the rubbery corners on
your channel selector buttons:
three rows across, five rows down
with the power button set off alone to the right.

Oh, how I enjoy stroking your
nubile protrusions late at night
when my mind has turned to mush.
And how I relish the illusion of power you give me
as I hold the world in my hand.

At times I feel guilty.
I have let you become tarnished
and little almost imperceptible
colonies of mold have begun
to grow on you–probably as spores from the
tips of my fingers.

And one more thing– I'll say it right out.
I put you in my mouth.
I rub my teeth and gums with your corner and
I apologize to you for that
because I have made you–
a marvel of technology–
an unclean thing.

What If There Were No Birthdays

What if there were no birthdays
because nobody ever could say,
exactly what year they were born in,
or, more important, the day.

Would we celebrate unbirthdays forever?
Would society grind to a stop?
Would partiers forget whose unbirthday it was
and walk around dazed?–I think not.

If there were no birthday celebrations
you could grow old without much ado.
When you learned how to walk would be Walk Day,
and when you learned how to run you'd be two.

If there were no presents required
and hair started growing on your cheek,
you'd tell all the world it was Fuzz Day,
then try growing a beard for the week.

The sun would consistently rise in the east
and the moon would encircle the earth.
The constellations would move very slowly
while giving only a hint of our birth.

The Cybernetic Possum

Some people get old in their twenties
just working themselves to the bone,
while others stay young in their sixties
without having much cares of their own.

So today is my happy unbirthday
though my body's not feeling as young
as it has on other unbirthdays,
yet there are many unbirthdays to come.

Who You Are

A young man asked me the other day
what to do and what to say.
I told him that before you go far
you've gotta know just who you are.

Your mom says this and your dad says that
and pretty soon you don't know where you're at,
so you look for the answer on your own
and end up living far from home.

Then you meet a girl and after you're caught,
it's "Good-bye sucker, you're not what I thought."
And you feel inside that you were a clown
so you spend some time just being down.

Then you ask yourself, because you can't hide,
"Is there anything here, left inside?"
As you sit on the stool in a dark, empty bar
knowing it ain't easy being who you are.

Poem Written On The Run

Gotta go shopping and get to work.
No time to sit here like a jerk
trying to find some words that rhyme.
All I'm doing is wasting time.

The Real News

Seeing that Tom broke off, George willed
but Leslie stalled and started seeing Dan
rather than wasting time with Donald's son
who happened to be John's chancellor.

To Ram Dass

Ram Dass, Ram Dass, how do you do it!
You've been talking for forty some years
about how we humans are more than our egos,
how joy is a part of our tears.

Duality's just a part of illusion,
the many just part of the one.
Some say it's all just a form of delusion,
but I'd say you're still having fun.

THE HONEST THIEF

Was 'bout the time I hit the desert
and the sun was getting' hot.
I'll tell ya 'bout a guy I met,
about a ride I got.

His name was Jack, that's all I know,
and some would say he's mean,
cuz of the thirty years he lived,
he done time for near thirteen.

We had some dope and beer,
talked about his kid and wife,
and how he'd had to get away ,
to straighten out his life.

I never seen a man so pissed,
a man so bruised and sore.
Said when he felt the hate come on,
he'd rob a liquor store.

He told the judge, when he got caught,
before they locked his cell,
that if he didn't think it right,
then, "You can go to hell."

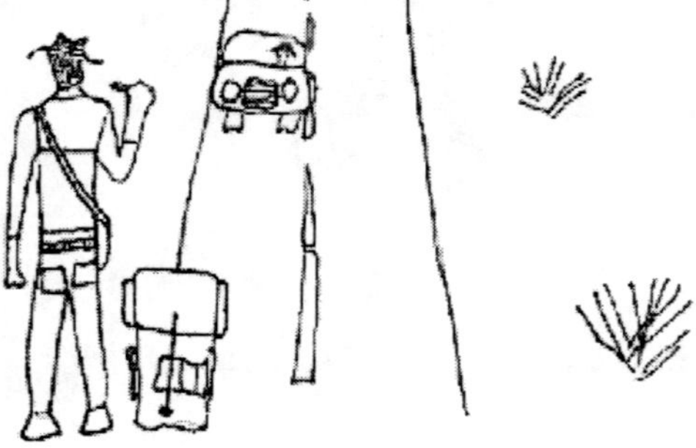

"Cuz I been to reform school,
an' I done served some time,
an' I been down and I been out,
an' I been feeling fine."

"I know I growed up rotten,
and you got your job to do
So take away a few more years...
ain't got nothin' left to loose."

Ole Jack was getting' mighty hot,
didn't care much if he died,
but one thing he convinced me of,
he weren't the kind that lied.

Now I met up with slippery dudes,
who give me lots of grief,
but when I looked at Jack that day,
I saw an honest thief.

The Cybernetic Possum

"You know," he said, "I hitched this road,
through rain and snow and drought
an, when I see a guy like you,
I always help him out."

"My wife she got some money,
her ol' man left her in his will."
Then he layed down on the seat,
a twenty dollar bill.

"I don't care what you do with it,
cuz money's always blind,
but if you meet a dude in need,
just do him somethin' kind."

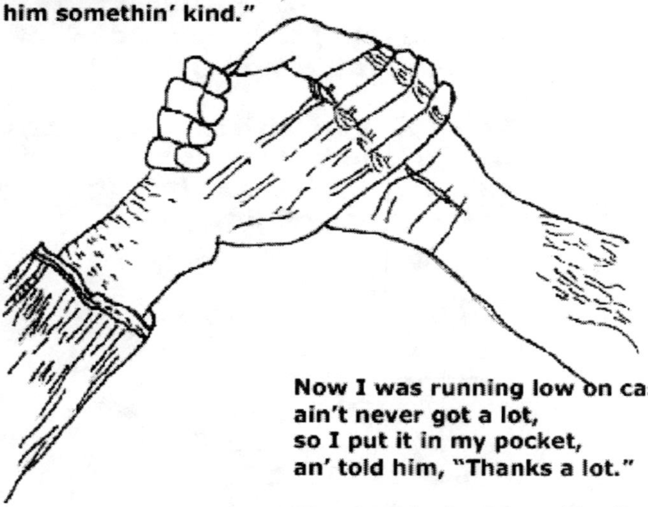

Now I was running low on cash,
ain't never got a lot,
so I put it in my pocket,
an' told him, "Thanks a lot."

The road he took was heading north,
but I was headed east.
We pulled into a truck stop,
and I had a little feast.

I never met his kind before,
but if I meet another,
I'll look him in the eye like Jack,
take his hand...and call him brother.

The Walter Cronkite Memorial Poem

Sitin' here with a broken heart,
waiting for the news to start,
sorry that we split apart.
Wondering why my baby left me,
left me with the blues.

Waiting for the clock to hit five-thirty,
feeling kind of low and dirty.
What we had was sweet and perty.
Wondering why my baby left me,
left me with the blues.

Got a letter in the mail,
said our love would surely fail,
said she'd really rather bail.
Wondering why my baby left me,
left me with the blues.

Come on Walter Cronkite,
tell me that it's all right.
Tell me why my baby left me,
left me with the blues.

A Tribute to Greg Knutson

Greg Knutson
1959 - 1996

A Tribute to Greg Knutson

I first met Greg Knutson while driving taxi at Union Cab Co-op in Madison, WI. He was a driver and dispatcher on the night shift and well on his way to a PhD in Mathematics at the University of Wisconsin. He was a National Chess Master and well as a self taught guitarist and amateur master of the ancient Chinese board game of Go.

Greg died on the night July 28, 1996 when he was run over by a truck on the interstate highway north of Madison. He was 37 years old. I remember Greg as a kind soul with a gentle sense of humor. He was slim and wore his dark hair in a pageboy cut with bangs in the front. He had a baritone radio voice and used to read selections of poetry over the air when he dispatched after business had slowed down. I became aware of his poetry only after he died when they were published in *Mobius,* a local literary magazine.

What follows are six of Greg's poems which exemplify the broad imagination and keen intellect of this Renaissance man. RC

A Conjecture of Partly Dave

By Greg Knutson

There's an unproved theorem
on the duality of
purpose
that spreads
like crabgrass
over outlandish
schemes.
It's about beats,
absolute zero
and vats of cement
held in wires
from cranes.
It's a periodic
table of the
elements of style,
a yellow tractor
with two sets
of mandibles
or joy beyond
weights and measure
like a friend at the grocery store
or big thighs
in the afternoon.

Poets Theme Park

By Greg Knutson

Somewhere there's a tiki-room
where klee birds just nod their heads
silently.

Somewhere there's a mountain
of rage,
rife with orange magma.

Somewhere there's a boardwalk
where hermits gamble for time.

Royalty

By Greg Knutson

Yesterday I paid a visit
to the city in the clouds
populated by finger-people.

I was granted
audience with the thumb king
who wore a silk robe colored
five-ball orange.

I can no longer
restrain my laughter when
I realize his eyes and
broad smile have been
drawn in magic marker.

Dear Mr. Science

By Greg Knutson

Despite recent advances in optics
there is no device which allows you
to see through the eyes of a child.
It's been 47 years, still no one's
repaired the sound barrier.
Furthermore
no matter how well you
master the language of dolphins
they will not invite you to
the secret ritual at
their underwater circle
of stones.

The Creation Fair

By Greg Knutson

The Children hunt for skulls
of early humanoids.
Thomas Aquinas has lunch in
the tent and orders primordial soup.
BOOM BOTTA BING!
The cosmic slot machine pays off
a 10 billion to one jackpot
while smiling bandits play
mariachi on twisted
xylophones of D.N.A.

Conventional Wisdom

By Greg Knutson

Bury a shoe, but put a glove
out to sea.
Never give a blue iris to
the village idiot before sunset.
Don't pirouette in a room
full of candles.

It's better to climb the volcano
alone at midnight than to
feed scallops to the three-headed dog
from hell.

Choose your last words…
very carefully.

LaVergne, TN USA
09 May 2010
182089LV00001B/26/P

9 780978 909314

About The Author

Richard Chamberlin has a BA in journalism from Columbia College and has been a newspaper reporter, free lance writer, psychiatric nurse, and cab driver. He lives in the small city of Monona just outside of Madison, Wisconsin with his wife.